THERE'S A MONSTER IN THE GARDEN

Poems by
DAVID HARMER

Drawings by
TIM ARCHBOLD

Frances Lincoln
Children's Books

CONTENTS

THE PRIME MINISTER IS TEN TODAY

This morning I abolished
homework, detention and dinner ladies.
I outlawed lumpy custard, school mashed spuds
and handwriting lessons.
From now on playtimes must last two hours
unless it rains, in which case we all go home
except the teachers, who must do extra PE
outside in the downpour.

Whispering behind your hand in class
must happen each morning between ten and twelve,
and each child only has to do
ten minutes' work in one school hour.

I've passed a No Grumpy Teacher law
so one bad word or dismal frown
from Mr Spite or Miss Hatchetface
will get them each a month's stretch
sharpening pencils and marking books
inside a gaol of their choice.

All headteachers are forbidden
from wearing soft-soled shoes.
Instead they must wear wooden clogs
so you can hear them coming.
They are also banned from shouting
or spoiling our assembly by pointing
at the ones who never listen.

Finally, all schools must shut
for at least half the year,
and if the weather's really sunny
the teachers have to take us all
to the seaside for the day,
and buy us ice-creams.

If you've got some good ideas
for other laws about the grown-ups
drop me a line in Downing Street,
I'll always be glad to listen.
Come on, help me change a thing or two.
Before we all grow up
and get boring.

PASS IT ON, IT'S REALLY TRUE!

Our headmaster, Mr Pugh
Kissed our teacher, sweet Miss Drew
Hannah had a perfect view
From outside the Y6 loo
Clare and Rachel saw it too
They told me, now I've told you.
Pass it on, it's really true.

Our bossy cook, Mrs Smew
Puts frogs and spiders in the stew
Mixes treacle tart with glue
And lizard's doo-doos from the zoo
Makes us eat the awful brew
Jack and Billy heard it too.
Pass it on, it's really true.

Did you know that it was James
Wrote on the school wall during games
With a pen he pinched from Sky?
She got told off, which made her cry
And Tim loves Jade and she loves Paul

Paul loves Clare who loves them all.
Pass it on, it's really true.

Kyle put paint in Kieron's shoe
When he was in the dinner queue
Kieron hasn't got a clue
Why his socks have turned bright blue
But thanks to me he soon knew
You see I told him it was you!
Pass it on, it's really true.

Pass it on, pass it on, pass it on,
It's really true!

ME

A bundle of quick-fire lightning explodes
Down the road as I run for school.

Arms and legs whizz and whir
Through iron gates, volcanoes of laughter
Erupting noisily with the bell.

A dinosaur is chewing lumps
Of meaty words and chunky numbers,
Maps and magnets, a diet of dates.

On the yard bloodthirsty Vikings
Win at football then drag their longships
Up soft beaches of art and singing.

Until a boffin with seven brains
Bursts into the computer room
To launch his fleet of rockets.

A slippery snail struggles up
A long-haul hill of homework.
Inky blots like squirmy worms
Wriggle on the paper.

The clock stops, batteries fail,
The moon shuts down through a long dark night.
I fall asleep and dream
Of pirates sailing the stormy seas.

Toast! Tea! Juice! Breakfast!
Fuel me up, it's another day.
Open the door for this blur of a boy
Barging his way to school.

SOME DAYS

Some days this school
is a huge concrete sandwich
squeezing me out like jam.

It weighs so much
breathing hurts, my legs freeze,
my body is heavy.

On days like that
I carry whole buildings
high on my back.

Other days
the school is a rocket
thrusting right into the sun.

It's yellow and green
freshly painted,
the cabin windows
gleam with laughter.

On days like that
whole buildings support me,
my ladder is pushing
over their rooftops.

Among the clouds
I'd need a computer
to count all the bubbles
bursting aloud in my head.

MAGIC THE RABBIT

My rabbit is called Magic.
Not just because he wrinkles his nose
And carrots disappear.

Not just because
He wriggles right under the straw
At the back of his hutch
And he disappears.

Not just because
Every time my football team wins
He leaps up and down.

But because last week
He turned the milkman into a frog
The paper girl into a walrus
The postman into a purple jelly
The dustman into a giant banana,
And made my mum and dad
King and Queen of all the world
And me Prime Minister.

'That's magic, Magic,' we cheered
Once he wished them all back again.
'Really magic.'

MISTER MOORE

Mister Moore, Mister Moore
Creaking down the corridor.

Uh eh uh uh eh
Uh eh uh uh eh

Mister Moore wears wooden suits
Mister Moore has great big boots
Mister Moore's got his hair like a brush
And Mister Moore don't like me much.

Mister Moore, Mister Moore
Creaking down the corridor.

Uh eh uh uh eh
Uh eh uh uh eh

When my teacher's there I haven't got a care
I can do my sums, I can do gerzinters
Mister Moore comes through the door
Got a wooden head full of splinters.

Mister Moore, Mister Moore
Creaking down the corridor.

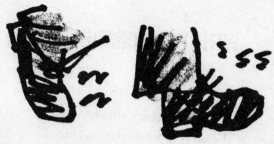

Uh eh uh uh eh
Uh eh uh uh eh

Mister Moore I implore
My earholes ache, my head is sore
Don't come through my classroom door
Don't come through my classroom door.

Mister Moore, Mister Moore
Creaking down the corridor.

Uh eh uh uh eh
Uh eh uh uh eh

Mister Moore wears wooden suits
Mister Moore has great big boots
Mister Moore's got his hair like a brush
And Mister Moore don't like me much.

Mister Moore, Mister Moore
Creaking down the corridor.

Uh eh uh uh eh
Uh eh uh uh eh

WINTER MORNING: WINTER NIGHT

This morning I walked to school
through the dark,
it was so cold my shadow shivered
under the street lamps.

My feet cracked the ice
that glittered as hard as the frosted stars
stuck on the sky's blue back.

Cars crept by like giant cats,
their bright eyes shining.

Tonight I walked over the snow,
the moon's cool searchlight
splashed its glow over the gardens.

Picking out details of rooftops and hedges
as clearly and sharply
as a summer stillness just after dawn.

Cats on the street roared like lions
bounding over the wet tarmac.

ON A BLUE DAY

On a blue day
when the brown heat
scorches the grass
and stings my legs with sweat,

I go running like a fool
up the hill towards the trees
and my heart beats loudly
like a kettle boiling dry.

I need a bucket the size of the sky
filled with cool, cascading water.

At evening
the cool air rubs my back,
I listen to the bees working for their honey

and the sunset pours light
over my head like a waterfall.

RUDOLPH'S STORY

Last night as we practised for Christmas
Old Santa got carried away.
Looping the loop over Yorkshire
He fell right out of the sleigh.

We saw him float down through the sky
As the town far below fell asleep.
We saw him open his parachute
Then land in a compost heap.

At last we found the right garden,
All we saw were his boots in the air.
It took a time, but he struggled free
With cabbage leaves stuck in his hair.

'I've lost all my keys!' he shouted,
'From my pocket during my fall.
The keys that open the workshop door.
Now Christmas won't happen at all!'

We started to dig through the compost.
The terrible smell made us sneeze.
We jumped a mile when a little voice said,
'Please, are you looking for these?'

She stood there holding some keys.
They glowed with Santa's power.
'I'm Hannah,' she said, 'here, take them back,
Then Santa, please have a shower.'

He clapped his hands and cried, 'Thank you.
Now I can fill up my sack.
I tell you what, Hannah, for a reward,
Jump onto Rudolph's back.'

She felt as light as a snowflake.
You should've heard us all yell.
We zoomed past the stars, halfway to Mars,
Happy, in spite of the smell.

On Christmas Eve we found Hannah
Fast asleep in her bed.
We left her sack bursting with gifts
And a note from Santa which said:

'Dear Hannah, you really saved Christmas.
It wasn't some wonderful dream.
From all of us here, we'll see you next year.
Welcome to Santa's team!'

TWO TRAFFIC WARDENS TALKING ON CHRISTMAS EVE

Nabbed any good ones yet?
Too right I have, a big fat geezer
with a white beard, wearing a red suit,
and he's only trying to park
some kind of open truck on a double yellow line.

So you says to him push off?
Too right I did, I says to him, 'Oi
what do you think you are playing at here old son, eh?
This is a restricted zone, you can't park that thing here
especially with all those animals.'

Animals? What animals?
Horrible great big deer things with vicious horns,
and he keeps laughing and saying, 'Ho Ho Ho!'
I says to him, 'You'll soon stop laughing
when I write out this parking ticket, old lad.'

Nice one Stan, so what happened then?
One of those nasty great deer things,
really ugly it was, with a shiny red hooter,
only goes and eats my parking ticket
and tries to eat the rest of the pad as well as my hat.

Cheeky so and so, I hope you told him what for.
I did, I can tell you, I says, 'Oi! What's your game then?'
And he turns round and goes 'Ho Ho Ho' back at me,
tells me he's some kind of van driver
with a load of kids' toys and stuff to deliver.

So what? A double yellow line's a double yellow line.
Exactly. I soon told him, silly old fool,
looked him straight in the eye and wrote out a ticket
on the back of a shopping list I had handy.
'Who do you think you are?' I said. 'Father Christmas?'

SIR JOHN IS IN HIS KEEP TONIGHT

The twelfth of December, 1231,
terrible snows, darkness, no sun,
the castle is cold, silent and grey,
I'm here on my own,
my wife and children far away
on a winter holiday.
I've spent all the morning jousting,
knocking knights off their horses,
then archery in the butts, some swordplay,
but I'm on my own tonight, of course.
I've got all my servants and soldiers,
the fires keep burning bright,
but I'm alone in the keep
on my own
tonight.

I can see them clearly,
swarming over the curtain wall,
flooding the inner bailey,
the thousand ghosts of the thousand Saxons
my father and his father
slaughtered daily.
The Saxons fought well, died hard,
look at them cover the castle's yard,
ghosts, grey in the moonlight,
bearded warriors of yesterday
coming for me
tonight.

HEALTHY EATING

Mondays we have apples
With their healthy crunch
And broccoli and cabbage
For our healthy lunch
It makes me feel so queasy
I get a stomach-ache.
And up there in the staffroom
They're all eating cake!

Playtime on a Tuesday
It's carrots by the score
We chomp them and we chew them
And nearly break our jaw
But you can bet one teacher
Has had a birthday bake.
And up there in the staffroom
They're all eating cake!

I don't drink pop but water
For my thirst to slake
And eating greasy food's
A dietary mistake

But you need to be a hero
Like Sir Francis Drake
To ignore the staffroom door
Hides an awful fake,
And I know that grown-ups
Make the rules to break
And they need their snacks
To keep themselves awake
But I really saw it
With my mates Jake and Blake.
Up there in the staffroom
They're all eating cake!

Wednesday it is oranges
Thursday tangerines
Friday it's bananas
Or sometimes Clementines
I'd rather have a burger
And a thick milkshake.
And up there in the staffroom
They're all eating cake!

WHEN MUM TAKES ME FOOTBALL TRAINING

Mum gets out her old bike and pedals like crazy
she makes me run to the park
I get red faced and breathless.
When we arrive we play one against one,
she picks up the football and kicks it hard
as high as a bird in the big blue sky
it floats up there like a lost balloon,
comes thundering down and I say to myself
'Do I dare head it? Do I? Yes!'
But I don't and I miss it, nearly fall over
and head it back on the fourth bounce,
better still trap it, twist past three defenders
and run like a dart for the penalty spot
draw back my foot and belt it for goal.
My mum does her arm-stretched, starfish-shaped-
leap-like-a-cat save, and tips it just round the post,
we sit and laugh, then buy an ice-cream
take our time going home.

WHEN DAD TOOK ME FOOTBALL TRAINING

He put on his new trainers
he put on his new jogging bottoms
he put his fancy new football
in the car with the dog,
we drove to the park three streets away.
I got out and went in goal
I stood there for ages,
Dad kicked the ball
the dog pushed it back,
Dad toe-poked the ball
the dog shoved it back,
Dad tapped the ball
the dog rolled it back.
The sun came out. The dog rolled over.
Dad lay on the grass and went to sleep.
I flicked the ball on my right foot with my left
kept it off the ground for twenty-five kicks,
it dropped from my chest to my knee to my foot
I booted it hard into Dad's back
he grunted,
which woke the dog and it barked down his ear
so we all got into the car
and drove home.

DIWALI

Winter stalks us
like a leopard in the mountains
scenting prey.

It grows dark
bare trees stick black bars
across the moon's silver eye.

I will light my lamp for you
Lakshimi
drive away the darkness.

Welcome you into my home
Lakshimi
beckon you from every window.

With light that blazes
out like flames
across the sombre sky.

Certain houses
crouch in shadow, do not hear
your gentle voice.

Will not feel
your gentle heartbeat
bring prosperity and fortune.

Darkness hunts them
like a leopard in the mountains
stalking prey.

SORRY MUM!

Sorry Mum, sorry Mum
I'm really really sorry Mum!

I think I've lost the telly's remote
in the wheelie-bin, ripped my coat
on those railings in the park
didn't see the spikes it was so dark.

And of course there is the question
of laughing at Grandma's indigestion
she rocked the room when she burped
dropped her teeth in the tea she'd slurped.

Sorry Mum, sorry Mum
I'm really really sorry Mum!

I've flushed your mobile down the toilet
I really didn't mean to spoil it
I was only trying to get it clean
but now it is a submarine!

I smashed the mirror in the hall
juggling with my cricket ball
it cracked the glass and that was that
so, of course, I blamed the cat.

Sorry Mum, sorry Mum
I'm really really sorry Mum!

And I have to tell you, Mother
when I bound and gagged my brother
I gave him small electric shocks
by sticking wires through his socks.

The other end led to a socket
he leapt and jumped up like a rocket,
he nearly made it to the moon
I'm sure that he'll get better soon.

Sorry Mum, sorry Mum
I'm really really sorry Mum!

So when you told me off last night
I had a think and yes you're right
to yell at me and it sounded
like you mean it and I'm grounded.

So here's a present and a card
for when I've made your life so hard
I hope you have a lovely day
So now can I go out to play?

Sorry Mum, sorry Mum
I'm really really sorry Mum!

WHAT THE MOUNTAINS DO

What the mountains do is
roar silent warnings over
huge brown and heather-covered spaces

or fill up valleys with dark green laughter

before resting their stone-cropped heads
in sunlight.

OUR TREE

It takes so long for a tree to grow
So many years of pushing the sky.

Long branches stretch their arms
Reach out with their wooden fingers.

Years drift by, fall like leaves
From green to yellow then back to green.

Since my grandad was a boy
And then before his father's father

There's been an elm outside our school
Its shadow long across our playground.

Today three men ripped it down.
Chopped it up. It took ten minutes.

DOBBO'S FIRST SWIMMING LESSON

Dobbo's fists
spiked me to the playground wall
nailed me to the railings.

The plastic ball
he kicked against my skinny legs
on winter playtimes

bounced a stinging red-hot bruise
across the icy tarmac.
The day we started swimming
we all jumped in
laughed and splashed, sank beneath
the funny-tasting water.
Shivering in a corner
Dobbo crouched, stuck to the side
sobbing like my baby brother does
when all the lights go out.

CATS ARE COOL BUT DOGS ARE DUMB

Five cool cats on a roof in a row
Strut their stuff to the dog below
The dog goes mad, leaps at them all
Just like a canine cannon-ball.

Chorus:
Dogs
Woof woof woof
I'm rough and tough

Cats
Mee-ow mee-ow
No way, no how

Five cool cats drop to the ground
The dog bounces over in one bound
They flick their tails and silently
Flow like shadows up a tree.

Chorus

Five cool cats in a feline escape
The dog goes barking, it goes ape
The cats don't care, they just smile
Stretch out their legs to nap awhile.

Chorus

Five cool cats, they can't lose
The poor old dog is real bad news
Cats are clever, here they come
Dogs are lovely but they're dumb.

Chorus

GOOD MORNING!

It's my first morning away from home
my first morning in this hotel
I slept really well, so did Teddy
once we had dropped off to sleep
around three in the morning
because Darren and Brett kept laughing
Ben was snoring
and James was whispering scary ghost stories,
but now I'm awake
so I've put on my new jogging bottoms
my new T shirt, my new jacket
my new gloves, my baseball hat
and my cagoule,
I'm ready for anything, even though today
is the fourth of June
and the morning sun is shining over the sea
in flat golden patches
where gulls bob and swoop
and cry like babies
and everywhere is still and calm and peaceful,
mainly because it's half past six in the morning
and breakfast isn't until eight o'clock
there's nothing to do,
so I'll sing very loudly, wake everyone up
see if the teachers slept well like me.

SIR GUY AND THE ENCHANTED PRINCESS

Through howling winds on a storm-tossed moor
Sir Guy came to a castle door.

He was led by some strange power
To the deepest dungeon of a ruined tower.

A princess sat on a jewelled throne,
Her lovely features carved in stone.

His body trembled, was she dead?
Then her sweet voice filled his head.

'These evil spirits guard me well.
Brave Sir Knight, please break their spell.

Though I am stone, you shall see,
Kiss me once, I shall be free.'

As demons howled she came to life,
Blushed and whispered, 'Have you a wife?'

'My love,' he said, 'still remains
With collecting stamps and spotting trains.

But as long as you do as you're told
I think you'll do, come on, it's cold.'

'Oh,' she cried, 'you weedy bore,
I wish I was entranced once more.'

Lightning struck, the demons hissed.
Sir Guy was stone, a voice croaked, 'Missed!'

The princess rode his horse away
And poor Sir Guy's still there today.

BARRY'S BUDGIE...BEWARE

Dave's got a dog the size of a lion,
Half-wolf, half-mad, frothing with venom,
It chews up policemen and then spits them out.
But it's nothing to the bird I'm talking about.

Claire's got a cat as wild as a cheetah,
Scratching and hissing, draws blood by the litre,
Jumps high walls and hedges, fights bears on its own.
But there's one tough budgie it leaves well alone.

Murray my eel has teeth like a shark,
Don't mess with Murray, he'll zap out a spark.
But when Barry's budgie flies over the houses
Murray dims down his lights and blows his own fuses.

This budgie's fierce, a scar down its cheek,
Tattoos on its wings, mad screams in its beak,
Squawks wicked words, does things scarcely legal.
Someone should tell Barry he's got an eagle.

THERE'S A MONSTER IN THE GARDEN

If the water in your fish pond fizzes and foams
And there's giant teeth marks on the plastic gnomes
You've found huge claw prints in the flowerbed
And just caught sight of a two-horned head
Put a stick on your front lawn with a bit of card on
Look out everybody – there's a monster in the garden.

You haven't seen the dustman for several weeks
Haven't seen the gasman, he was looking for leaks
Haven't seen the paper-girl, postman or plumber
Haven't seen the window cleaner since last summer
Don't mean to be nosy, I do beg your pardon
Look out everybody – there's a monster in the garden.

One dark night it'll move in downstairs
Start living in the kitchen, take you unawares
Frighten you, bite on you, with howls and roars
It'll crash and smash about, shove you out of doors
In the cold and snow, the ice and rain will harden
Look out everybody – there's a monster in the garden.

Now listen to me neighbour, all of this is true
It happened next door, now it's happening to you
There's something nasty on the compost heap
Spends all day there curled up asleep
You don't want your bones crunched or jarred on
Look out everybody – there's a monster in the garden.

MY DAD'S A STUNTMAN

Some dads work on buses,
others work on trains
or pound the beat with great flat feet
or mend and clean the drains.

Some dads dig with shovels,
others sail the sea,
some are cooks, or publish books,
have chat shows on TV.

But my dad
jumps off the top of a giant skyscraper, lands
THUMP on a car roof, rolls over and leaps
through a stack of blazing tyres, dives
onto a motorbike and roars up the road.

Some dads sing in choirs,
others play guitars,
some have naps or gaze at maps
of planets, moons and stars.

Some dads play at football,
others like to draw,
some relax with books of facts
or paint the kitchen door.

But my dad
sleeps curled up on a bed of rusty nails, swims
across an icy pool a hundred times before breakfast,
sets fire to himself and falls out of a plane.
All in a day's work to my dad.

WILL IT GO TO A REPLAY?

Last night's cup-tie
West Ham and Sheffield United
was so exciting, really tough.

Two teams battled it out
through the rain and mud
as goal after goal
thudded into the net.

The crowd went wild
just loved
every nail-biting moment.

Four-four
with five minutes left
of extra time
both teams down to nine men
and the tension tightening.

In those dying minutes
both sides
cleared their goal lines
with desperate headers.

The Hammers missed a penalty
Blades missed an open goal.

With seconds to go
a replay at Bramall Lane
seemed certain, until
West Ham had to go in for her tea
and Sheffield United went to the shops
for his mum.

ALONE

The sun has been punctured,
Sagged out of sight behind the clouds.

I'm alone in the house
Watching the moon lay long cold fingers

Onto the curtains and through the glass
In the creaking windows.

If the footsteps outside come up the path
I'm going to hide under my bed.

If the hand I can hear tapping a key
Turns the lock and opens the door,

I'm going to scamper along the landing
Shove the bolt tight inside the bathroom.

If the voice I can hear breathing hard
Hisses and whispers up the stairs,

In those dying minutes
both sides
cleared their goal lines
with desperate headers.

The Hammers missed a penalty
Blades missed an open goal.

With seconds to go
a replay at Bramall Lane
seemed certain, until
West Ham had to go in for her tea
and Sheffield United went to the shops
for his mum.

ALONE

The sun has been punctured,
Sagged out of sight behind the clouds.

I'm alone in the house
Watching the moon lay long cold fingers

Onto the curtains and through the glass
In the creaking windows.

If the footsteps outside come up the path
I'm going to hide under my bed.

If the hand I can hear tapping a key
Turns the lock and opens the door,

I'm going to scamper along the landing
Shove the bolt tight inside the bathroom.

If the voice I can hear breathing hard
Hisses and whispers up the stairs,

In those dying minutes
both sides
cleared their goal lines
with desperate headers.

The Hammers missed a penalty
Blades missed an open goal.

With seconds to go
a replay at Bramall Lane
seemed certain, until
West Ham had to go in for her tea
and Sheffield United went to the shops
for his mum.

ALONE

The sun has been punctured,
Sagged out of sight behind the clouds.

I'm alone in the house
Watching the moon lay long cold fingers

Onto the curtains and through the glass
In the creaking windows.

If the footsteps outside come up the path
I'm going to hide under my bed.

If the hand I can hear tapping a key
Turns the lock and opens the door,

I'm going to scamper along the landing
Shove the bolt tight inside the bathroom.

If the voice I can hear breathing hard
Hisses and whispers up the stairs,

I'm going to scramble down the drainpipe
And run for cover in the back garden.

Monsters are clever, these two for example
Set their trap by calling my name

In the exact voice of my dad home from work
And of Mum back from the shops.

But I know their tricks, they won't catch me,
Although I suppose not many monsters

Bang and kick on the bathroom door
Yelling, 'Why at eleven years of age

Do we have to go through this nonsense
Each time one of us nips to the shops?'

Perhaps I've got it wrong
Again.

LION

Great rag bag
jumble-headed thing
shakes its mane
in a yawn that turns to anger,
teeth picked out like stalactites
in some vast cave,
bone-grinders, flesh-rippers,
hyena-bringers, jackal-callers,
and huge paws the size of death
clamp down on an antelope.
Later, sleeping through the night,
each star a lion
flung with pride across a sky
black as a roaring mouth,
lion dreams of open spaces,
dreams the smell of freedom.

MY MUM'S PUT ME ON THE TRANSFER LIST

On offer:
one nippy striker, ten years old
has scored seven goals this season
has nifty footwork and a big smile
knows how to dive in the penalty box
can get filthy and muddy within two minutes
guaranteed to wreck his kit each week.
This is a FREE TRANSFER
but he comes with running expenses
weeks of washing, shirts and shorts
socks and vests, a pair of trainers
needs to scoff huge amounts
of chips and burgers, beans and apples
pop and cola, crisps and oranges
endless packets of chewing gum.
This offer is open until the end of the season
I'll have him back then
at least until the cricket starts.
Any takers?

AT CIDER MILL FARM

I remember my uncle's farm
Still in midsummer,
Heat hazing the air above the red rooftops,
Some cattle sheds, a couple of stables
Clustered round a small yard
Lying under the hills that stretched their long back
Through three counties.

I rolled with his dogs
Among the hay bales
Stacked high in the barn he built himself
During a storm one autumn evening,
Tunnelled for treasure or jumped with a scream
From a pirate ship's mast into the straw,
Burrowed for gold and found he'd buried
Three battered Ford cars deep in the hay.

He drove an old tractor that sweated oil
In long black streaks down the rusty orange,
It chugged and whirred, coughed into life
Each day as he clattered across the cattle grids.
I remember one night my cousin and I
Dragging back cows from over the common.
We prodded the giant steaming flanks,
Pushed them homeward through the rain
And then drank tea from huge tin mugs,
Feeling like farmers.

He's gone now, he sold it,
But I have been back for one last look,
To the twist in the lane that borders the stream
Where Mary, Ruth and I once waded,
Water sloshing over our wellies,
And I showed my own children my uncle's farm,
The barn still leaning over the straw,
With for all I know three battered Ford cars
Still buried beneath it.

FELT PEN ALIENS

Squeak squeak squeak
Been hearing it all week
Red blue black
All waiting to attack.

You think I'm crazy but it's true
The felt-tip pens are after you.
Hear what I say, it isn't lies,
They are aliens in disguise,
On the whiteboard hear them squeaking,
It is just their way of speaking.
Let me translate, it means 'Let's go
And scribble out the earth below.'

Yes all those felt-pens up in space
Want to scribble on your face,
On your body, on your clothes,
They will scrawl right up your nose,
They'll write on you and your granny,
Cousin Bill and sister Annie.
You will be eliminated,
Those aliens will be elated.

If you're wanting to survive,
The moment they all come alive,
To give yourself a chance, a hope,
You'd better carry extra soap.
Be prepared to scrub and scour,
On each hour dive in the shower,
Wash off that ink from ear to ear
Before you start to disappear.

A silver spaceship's up there waiting
And it is anticipating
Earth's collapse, an invasion
By the felt-tip alien nation.
So many people have ignored
This warning, thought they could afford
To laugh at me and say I'm wrong.
Where are they now? Gone. Gone. Gone.

Squeak squeak squeak
Been hearing it all week
Red blue black
All waiting to attack.

GREAT GRAN IS MANIC ON HER MOTORBIKE

Shout out loud, say what you like
Great Gran is manic on her motorbike.

Last week her helmet touched the stars
As she zoomed over thirty cars
She didn't quibble, didn't fuss
When they added a double-decker bus.

Shout out loud, say what you like
Great Gran is manic on her motorbike.

She's a headline-hunting, bike-stunting
Wacky wild one-woman show
She revs and roars to wild applause
There is no place her bike won't go
She gives them shivers jumping rivers
And balancing along high wires
With a cheer she changes gear
Flies her bike through blazing tyres.

Shout out loud, say what you like
Great Gran is manic on her motorbike.

She told me when she quits bike-riding
She's going to take up para-gliding
I'll always be her favourite fan
My dazzling, daredevil, manic Great Gran!

Shout out loud, say what you like
Great Gran is manic on her motorbike.

NOW YOU TELL ME!

I think it's time that I should mention
Said my grandad
Sitting in his favourite chair
Winking one eye and tapping
A finger on the side of his nose.

That really I'm from Outer Space
Born on Neptune, moved to Pluto
Came down here
About three thousand years ago.

You daft old brush
Shouted my grandma from the kitchen,
Telling the boy
Your stupid stories
You've always lived on another planet
If you ask me.

Very true whispered my grandad
As a small, green eye
Flicked open on his forehead
And ten small claws
Slid out from under his nails
And wings the size of an eagle's
Flapped from his back
And vanished.

Very true indeed
Said my grandad
Sitting in his favourite chair
Tapping his nose
With a finger, winking
A cold eye as old as the mountains.

FROSTY PINCHFACE

Old Frosty Pinchface on the garden wall,
Shrivelled up and nasty, no fun at all,
Winter-filled eyes and a stone-cold stare,
Moonlight on his face, silver in his hair.

Old Frosty Pinchface, hear his bones crack,
A torn ragged coat and a hat so black,
Long pointy nose with a drip at its tip,
He's squeezing up the darkness in his icy grip.

Old Frosty Pinchface dances down the street,
Turns it to an iceberg stealing all the heat,
Scattering crystals of ice and snow,
Starting up his glacial, ice-floe show.

Old Frosty Pinchface seizes all he sees,
Houses start to shiver, hear the trees wheeze,
He freezes up the rivers, the valleys, the streams,
He freezes up your heart, your hopes, your dreams.

Old Frosty Pinchface, foul foggy breath,
Fingers like icicles poking us to death,
Horrid hoarse whispers chill us to the core.
Leave us alone, we don't need you any more!

Old Frosty Pinchface, tomorrow has begun,
Look who's arrived, our friend the Sun,
He's melting all your malice, oh yes it's true,
So get lost, off you go, before he melts you!

IT'S BEHIND YOU

I don't want to scare you
But just behind you
Is a..........................

No! Don't look!
Just act calmly
As if it wasn't there.

Like I said
Can you hear me if I whisper?
Just behind you
Is a...............................

NO! DON'T LOOK!
Just keep on reading
Don't turn round
It isn't worth it.

If you could see
What I can see standing there
You'd understand.

It's probably one
Of the harmless sort
Although with that mouth
Not to mention the teeth
And all that blood
Dripping down its chin
I wouldn't like to say.

DON'T TURN ROUND!
Listen
It's trying to speak
I think it wants to be friends.

Oh, I see it doesn't, never mind
You'd better leave just in case
I expect you'll escape
If you don't look round.

Oh, what a shame!
I thought you'd make it
To the door.
Hard luck
I still think it means no harm
I expect it eats all its friends.

FLIGHT FROM PLANET EARTH

Landing here because we had to,
the fuel gone and the computers broken,
we crashed into a bank of sand,
let the dust die down
then climbed out of our rocket.

We were surrounded by eyes
along the rim of the distant mountains
in the desert at our feet,
it was worse at night
when they glowed like fires
staring at us without blinking.

Time has passed.
We live in the wreck of our spacecraft,
eat what is left of our stores,
drink rainwater,
sometimes we go looking for food.
The creatures always force us back,
make us afraid.
We are the aliens here
and they don't like us.

A FEVER

I've got A fever
So, aardvarks, aeroplanes, apes and antelopes,
aerosols, anteaters, aspirins and Action Men,
acorns, alligators, aliens and astronauts,
asteroids, acrobats, angles and amplifiers
all make me itch and sneeze and cough.

My brother Zak's got Z fever,
can't go to the zoo, or subtract zero,
can't cross on a zebra, sneezes at zig-zags,
zips and zeitgeists, zeniths and zodiacs,
can't even say his own name.

My auntie Julie's got Y fever,
Hates Yorkies, yoghurt, yachts and yule logs,
yokes and yawning, yeast and yellowhammers,
comes out in a rash when somebody says
'I saw you yesterday you know.'

Uncle Jack has B fever,
Sister Dawn has E fever,
Cousin Masefield has C fever,
But me, I've got A fever.

So, artichokes, A-levels, albums and antibodies,
alloys, aviaries, all-spice and armpits,
admin, admen, admirals and allegories,
all make me itch, cough and sneeze.
Can't even watch Andy Pandy or the A Team,
cos me, I've got A fever.
Achoooo!

THE VISITOR

It was late last night I'm certain
Wasn't it?
That I saw my bedroom curtain
Twitch and flutter
Felt a chill, heard him mutter
'Hello lad, I'm back.'

Uncle Jack
Dead since this night last year
Wasn't it?
A pickled onion in his beer
Stopped his breath, a sudden death
That took us sadly by surprise.

But there he was, those eyes
One grey, one blue
One through
Which the light could pass
The other, glass.

He drifted down, swam about
Didn't he?
In his brown suit, flat cap, stout
Boots and tie,
I saw him remove the eye
Didn't I?

'It's not a dream,
This,' he said, 'don't scream,
I'll not come back, I shan't return.'
Then I felt the ice-cold burn
Of his glass eye on my skin,
Saw his ghastly, ghostly grin.
'Don't worry, don't get in a stew.
Just thought I'd keep an eye on you!'

When I woke up today
I saw the blue eye not the grey,
But when I picked it up to go
It drained away like melting snow.
Didn't it?

I ONCE MET A PIRATE

I once met a pirate on old Whitby Dock
A long rusty cutlass, a battered flintlock
Stuck in his belt as he gazed out to sea
I coughed and he turned, said this to me.

'Now then young shaver, you look a bright lad
And I know a ship with a berth to be had
She's called *The Bright Star*, she's out in the bay
Taking on crew, you could sign up today!

She's got a black flag, a skull and crossed bones
And she'll keep you safe from old Davy Jones
Sleek as a bird on the oceans she'll glide
With you in the crow's nest riding the tide.

If you want adventure, treasure and gold
A life that is careless, carefree and bold
Be richer than kings, be happy and free
Just climb aboard, be a pirate like me.

Here's my old parrot, he's called Mr Squawk
Sailed every sea-lane from here to New York
Under his wing, lad, is where you belong
With him on your shoulder you cannot go wrong.

Feel the waves tumble, there's salt in the air
Wind fills the canvas, the weather is fair
Wish by the stars and Saturn's dark moons
You'll soon get your fill of gems and doubloons!'

Then out of the crowds my father appeared
'Don't talk to yourself, son, stop acting weird
There's nobody there, just ships and the shore
You foolish young boy, you're dreaming once more.'

There wasn't anything much I could say
He gave me a push and we walked away
But turning my head I looked at the quay
And there was my pirate waving at me.

Don't care what you think, don't care what is said
He wasn't a phantom, some ghost in my head
I'll never forget as I wind my life's clock
The pirate I met on old Whitby Dock.

DAZZLING DEREK

That's my dad shouting at me
from the touchline
like he does every game we play.

I don't know why
I think we do quite well really
this week we're only losing ten-one
and I've scored three times
twice in my goal once in theirs.

Not bad for a goalie.

Last week I was on the wing
it was brilliant
I nearly scored a million times
we still lost but who was counting?

My dad was,
he got really angry,
there's no pleasing him.

What he really wants to do
is to shrink back to being ten like me
slip onto the field, score the winning goal
with seconds to go
defeat staring us in the face
Dazzling Derek saves the day!

But he can't
so he jumps up and down on the touchline
shouts at me
mutters and kicks the grass
stubs his toe and yells
nearly gets sent off the field by the ref.

Where's the fun in that?

ALL OF US KNOCKING ON THE STABLE DOOR

Three great kings, three wise men,
Tramp across the desert to Bethlehem,
Arrive at the inn, travel no more,
We start knocking on the stable door.

Knocking at the door, knocking at the door
All of us are knocking on the stable door.

I've got myrrh, he's got gold,
He's got frankincense and all of us are cold,
We stand here shivering, chilled to the core,
We're just knocking on the stable door.

The star above it glows in the sky,
Burning up the darkness and we know why.
A baby king's asleep in the straw
So we start knocking on the stable door.

Travelled some distance, we've travelled far,
Melchior, Caspar and Balthazaar.
We are so wealthy, the baby's so poor
But here we are knocking on the stable door.

Now is the time, now is the hour
To feel the glory, worship the power.
We quietly enter, kneel on the floor
Just the other side of the stable door.

Knocking at the door, knocking at the door
All of us are knocking on the stable door.
Knocking at the door, knocking at the door
We're all knocking on the stable door.

LIVING WITH CATS

The cat's shadow
stretches a thin dark rope
along the white wall.

And the shrew
snuffles the scent
through its long thin nose.

Knows what it senses.

Goes jittering
　　　skittering

with not enough legs
to escape.

***

Next door's spaniel
is going ballistic

completely baking

cats in the sun
lazy as lions on the garage roof
wave their tails.

Next door's spaniel
must be a springer

up and down
on his pogo-stick legs
howling and snarling
like a pack of bloodhounds.

Cats in the shade
half asleep on next door's patio
stick out their tongues.

***

Masie and Piglet
have tracked down the doormat
stalked the slidy-slippery rug
and pounced on the carpet.

Those jobs are done
no more trouble there.

Now they are watching the tropical fish tank
like some giant television,
they are waiting for the channel to change
to their favourite programme

scuba-diving for kittens.

***

Quickly and quietly
the cat crosses
the great green river
of the settee.

Paw to paw
avoiding the water
by delicate leaps

on the stepping stones
of our sleeping heads.

LOST IN SPACE

When the spaceship first landed
nose down in Dad's prize vegetables
I wasn't expecting the pilot
to be a large blue blob with seven heads
the size and shape of rugby balls.

'Is this Space Station Six?' he asked.
'No,' I said. 'It's our back garden, number fifty-two.'
'Oh,' he said. 'Are you sure?'
And took from his silver overalls
a shiny book of maps.

There were routes round all the galaxies
ways to the stars through deepest space
maps to planets I'd never heard of
maps to comets, maps to moons
and short-cuts to the sun.

'Of course,' he said. 'Silly me,
I turned left not right at Venus.
Easily done, goodbye.'
He shook his heads, climbed inside,
the spaceship roared into the sky
and in a shower of leeks and cabbages
disappeared for ever.

WHO IS MY NEIGHBOUR?

From Jerusalem to Jericho
The road was lonely, narrow, slow.

A man came walking down the track
As thieves crept up behind his back.

They knocked him down and beat his head
Stripped him, robbed him, left him for dead.

He lay there bleeding in the dirt
Moaning, groaning, badly hurt.

The sun burned down, his throat ran dry
But then a priest came passing by.

'Water please,' cried out the man
'Priest help me any way you can.'

No help came, he was denied
The priest walked by on the other side.

A second priest ignored his plight
Just walked away and out of sight.

As a Samaritan drew near
He shouted out in pain and fear.

'My wife and children grieve for me
I am in the hands of my enemy.'

But with those hands his wounds were bathed
They raised him up and he was saved.

Carried as a donkey's load
To an inn along the road.

Washed and bandaged, laid to sleep
Two silver coins left for his keep.

'Take care of him,' said his new friend
'I'll pay whatever else you spend

And when he wakes let him know
I was his neighbour not his foe.'

ALIEN EXCHANGE

We've got an alien at our school
he's on an exchange trip
I'd quite fancy him
if he wasn't so weird-looking.
Just one head
only two legs
and no feelers at all,
he hasn't got claws on the end of his hands
and he's only got—don't laugh—two eyes.

Can you believe that?
When we first saw him we fell about
but as our teacher says
we must be thoughtful and respect all visitors
to our galaxy,
even if they have only got one feeding system,
a breathing tube that is much too small
and horrid furry stuff on their head.

Next month my sister and I
are visiting his planet on the exchange.
It's got a funny name, Earth.
We've got to stay two weeks.
Our teacher says we must be careful
not to tread on the Earthlings by mistake
and always, always be polite,
to raise our wings in greeting
and to put rubber tips on our sharpest horns.
I'm not looking forward to it much,
the food looks awful
and the sea's dirty, not to mention the air.
Still. It'll make a change from boring old school
and perhaps some alien
will quite fancy me!

SLICK NICK'S DOG'S TRICKS

Slick Nick's dog does tricks
The tricks Nick's dog does are slick
He picks up sticks, stands on bricks
Nick's finger clicks, the dog barks SIX!
He picks a mix of doggy bix
Then gives Slick Nick thick sloppy licks
Mick and Rick's dog's not so quick
Kicks the bricks, drops the sticks
Can't bark to six, is in a fix
Gets on their wicks, despite its mix
Of waggy tail and loving licks
But Slick Nick's dog does tricks
The tricks Nick's dog does are slick.

PASTING PATSY'S PASTY POSTERS

Petra Porter pastes in precincts
Patsy's pasty pasties' posters
Patsy's posters from her pasties
And her tasty pasty pasta.

Patsy pays a pretty penny
For Petra's posters in the precincts
But Paula pastes her posters faster
Passes Petra pasting past her.

So Patsy's pasting Paula's posters
Paying pasty Paula plenty
For faster pasta poster pasting
Pasting pasta posters faster.

HARRY HOBGOBLIN'S SUPERSTORE

You want a gryphon's feather
Or a spell to change the weather?
A pixilating potion
To help you fly an ocean?
Some special brew of magic
To supercharge your broomstick?
Witches, wizards, why not pop
Into Harry's one-stop shop?

Tins of powdered dragon's teeth,
Bottled beetles, newts.
Freeze-dried cobwebs, cats and rats,
Screaming mandrake roots.
Lizard skins stirred widdershins,
A giant's big toe-nail,
Second-hand spells used only once,
New ones that can't fail.
Spells to grow a donkey's ears
On the teacher no one likes,
Spells to make you good at sums,
Spells to find lost bikes.

Spells that grow and stretch and shrink,
Spells that make your best friend stink,
Sacks of spells stacked on his shelves,
Come on in, see for yourselves.
Magical prices, tricks galore
At Harry Hobgoblin's Superstore.

STINKERMAN

I'm Stinkerman, yes, Stinkerman
Stinking like a frying pan
Full of fat that's six weeks old
Rancid, rotten, full of mould
I smell of socks soaked in cheese
Nasty cabbage and putrid peas
I pong of milk that has gone sour
That's the secret of my power!

You can tell by the ghastly smell
Oh no! It's Stinkerman
You can niff that dreadful whiff!
Oh no! It's Stinkerman.

Superman fears me more
Than green kryptonite
I paralyse his nerves with smells
That make him sick all night.
When Batman sniffs my odours
He has to find fresh air
Spiderman just runs away
And Robin isn't there.
Yes all these Superheroes
Are just a foolish sham
Just remember this–
I stink, therefore, I am!

You can tell by the ghastly smell
Oh no! It's Stinkerman
You can niff that dreadful whiff!
Oh no! It's Stinkerman.

ALL KINDS OF KIDS!

The batty and the chatty
The scatty and the catty
The dippy and the lippy
The gobby and the snobby
The loopy and the droopy
The soppy and the floppy
The feared and revered
The one with a beard!

The ones who run in races
The ones who pull daft faces
The smiley and the wily
The pretty and the gritty
The ones who jump about
The ones who like to shout
The squirmers and the squigglers
The weirdos and the gigglers.

The grotty and the snotty
The nerdy and the wordy
The dreamy and the screamy
The ones who make you weary
The ones who talk like crazy
The ones who are quite lazy
The ones we all adore
The ones who are a bore.

The wary and the scary
The freaky and the geeky
The cheery and the sneery
The stinky and the slinky
The spotty and the dotty
The lumpy and the grumpy
The ones who like to natter
The ones with chat-up patter.

All kinds of kids
Everyone unique
Every one matters
Every day and every week
Got to help each other
Got to pull through
Don't care if you don't like it
It's what you've got to do.

Long ago, David Harmer was a primary school headteacher so he knows a lot about monsters! After he stopped being a head monster he started working in schools and libraries all over the country, helping children and grown-ups to write poems and stories. Frequently, he worked with his friend Paul Cookson in their popular poetry duo, *Spill The Beans*.

David likes making people laugh and writing poems that everyone can join in with, as well as some more serious ones. He has published many poetry collections for children, as well as hundreds of poems in anthologies. He lives with his wife, Paula, in Doncaster, Yorkshire. They have two grown-up daughters, four cats and two dogs.

And a monster that lives in the garden.

MORE POETRY TITLES FROM
FRANCES LINCOLN CHILDREN'S BOOKS

An Imaginary Menagerie
9781847801661

Can It Be About Me?
9781847803405

Come Into This Poem
9781847801692

Cosmic Disco
9781847803986

Crazy Classrooms
9781847805058

Give Us a Goal!
9781847803412

Hey Little Bug!
9781847801685

Here Come the Creatures!
9781847803672

I'm a Little Alien!
9781847804815

I Am a Poetato
9781847806000

My Life as a Goldfish
9781847804822

The Dragon with a Big Nose
9781847803658

The Monster Sale
9781847803665

Werewolf Club Rules
9781847804525

You Tell Me
9781847804440

Frances Lincoln titles are available from all good bookshops.
You can also buy books and find out more about your favourite titles,
authors and illustrators on our website: www.franceslincoln.com